BACKBOARD ADMIRAL

DAVID ROBINSON

THE ACHIEVERS

DAVID
ROBINSON

BACKBOARD

ADMIRAL

Dawn M. Miller

Lerner Publications Company ▪ Minneapolis

This book is available in two editions:
Library binding by Lerner Publications Company
Soft cover by First Avenue Editions
241 First Avenue North
Minneapolis, Minnesota 55401

To Conrad, for his subtle encouragement,
and to Tracy, for his interest in books

LIBRARY OF CONGRESS CATALOGING-IN-PUBLICATION DATA

Miller, Dawn M.
    David Robinson : backboard admiral / Dawn M. Miller.
        p.   cm.—(The Achievers)
    Summary: Profiles the college and professional basketball
career of the U.S. Naval Academy graduate who entered the
National Basketball Association in 1989 after completing two
years with the Navy.
    ISBN 0-8225-0494-4 (lib. bdg.)
    ISBN 0-8225-9600-8 (pbk.)
    1. Robinson, David, 1965-   —Juvenile literature. 2. Basket-
ball players—United States—Biography—Juvenile literature.
[1. Robinson, David, 1965-   . 2. Basketball players. 3. Afro-
Americans—Biography.] I. Title. II. Series.
GV884.R615M55   1991
796.323'092—dc20
[B]
[92]   90-44936
                                                               CIP
                                                                AC

Manufactured in the United States of America

International Standard Book Number: 0-8225-0494-4 (lib. bdg.)
International Standard Book Number: 0-8225-9600-8 (pbk.)
Library of Congress Catalog Card Number: 90-44936

2   3   4   5   6   7   8   9   10   00   99   98   97   96   95   94   93   92   91

Contents

David Robinson (50) made a big impact during his first year with the San Antonio Spurs.

1
Arriving in the NBA

When David Robinson landed in the National Basketball Association in 1989, he was an immediate sensation. Not only did he have tremendous potential as a 7-foot-1 center, but his background as a U.S. Naval Academy graduate drew the interest of basketball fans across the country.

During his college years, Robinson had been praised for his quickness and natural talent for basketball. Just as frequently, however, he had been criticized because people felt he wasn't dedicated to the game. After less-than-spectacular showings in the Olympics and other amateur competitions in the two years he had served in the Navy, people continued to doubt that Robinson could be a franchise player—one that his NBA team, the San Antonio Spurs, could build a winning team around. The Spurs did intend for Robinson to be their premier player.

The team had waited through two atrocious losing seasons for him, and management, players, and fans were counting on his ability to dominate basketball games. The battle cry in San Antonio for two years had been, "Wait until David comes!"

When the San Antonio Spurs made Robinson the first pick in the 1987 draft, Angelo Drossos was the owner of the team. He knew the team would have to wait until Robinson was out of the Navy before seeing him in a Spurs uniform. Drossos and the rest of the Spurs management felt Robinson was worth the wait.

In the two years since the Spurs had drafted Robinson, there had been a few changes in San Antonio. A new owner, Red McCombs, was rumored to be considering moving the team to another city. A new coach, Larry Brown, had requested several trades to strengthen the team. As a result, by the time Robinson joined the Spurs in the fall of 1989, only three players remained from the team's previous season.

Because Robinson had played so infrequently during his two years in the Navy, the Spurs had him play in summer rookie and professional leagues to help him get in shape and to introduce him to the style of game the pros play. "I had fun and I found the things that I needed to work on," Robinson said of the summer games. "I have to bring my whole game around. I'm a good player now, but you have to keep learning. There is always something more to learn."

Coach Larry Brown made several changes on the team to prepare for Robinson's arrival.

The eight-game exhibition schedule before the season began helped give Robinson an idea of the competition that he would face during the regular season. Judging from his performance against the other NBA teams, Robinson was prepared. He averaged 24.9 points and 9.6 rebounds per game, while shooting 51.1 percent from the field in the preseason.

Robinson's long wait finally ended on November 4, when the Spurs took on the Los Angeles Lakers in the opening game of the regular season. One sports newspaper reported that Robinson had an upset stomach and threw up during the opener. The ailment was a sign that he was indeed nervous, despite statements he made in the weeks leading up to the game.

He had said the pressure wasn't affecting him. Robinson joked that the upset stomach was caused by a bad Mexican meal he had eaten a week earlier.

Despite Robinson's jitters, his debut served notice that he had arrived in the NBA and that he had every intention of being a dominant player. He scored 23 points and had 17 rebounds to lead the Spurs to a 106–98 win over the Lakers. Yet Robinson's Navy background set him apart from the other players. One Spurs official took his wife to see the game, then asked her afterward what she liked most about Robinson. She replied, "The way he stood at attention for the national anthem."

The game also showed that teams weren't going to be able to take advantage of the one glaring weakness Robinson had shown in his game while at the Academy. In his first pro game, he made 11 of 14 free throws, proving his improvement at the line. He was also paid a tremendous compliment by Earvin "Magic" Johnson, a longtime All-Star guard for the Lakers. "Some rookies are never really rookies. Robinson's one of them," Johnson said.

Robinson's rookie year was exceptional. Not only did he exceed people's expectations that he would be the Rookie of the Year, but he helped his team win its first division title in seven years. The Spurs posted the best single-season improvement in NBA history by winning 35 more games than in the 1988–89 season.

Magic Johnson of the Lakers, like Robinson, was a great player as a rookie.

Basketball fans and the press liked Robinson because he was considerate, well-spoken, and intelligent.

Robinson also proved he could play with the best players in the league and more than hold his own against established centers like Patrick Ewing of the New York Knickerbockers and Hakeem Olajuwon of the Houston Rockets. David Robinson, nicknamed "the Admiral," had indeed arrived in the National Basketball Association.

Robinson was always good at sports, but he wasn't serious about basketball until after high school.

2
Growing into Basketball

The second child of Ambrose and Freda Robinson, David knew during his sophomore year of high school that he wanted to attend the United States Naval Academy at Annapolis, Maryland. At the time, his father was a senior chief sonar technician in the Navy.

Going to the Academy had several advantages. If he could make it through the tough military atmosphere and the competitive academic grind, David would receive an excellent education without having to pay tuition. He would also be guaranteed a job when he finished. Academy graduates earn a commission, or assignment, as a Navy or Marine Corps officer.

Robinson also considered the military atmosphere to be an advantage. "I was lazy in high school," he said. "I knew I was smart; things like math came really easy to me. I took advanced placement courses all the way through school, but I somehow didn't challenge myself." Robinson thought the Naval Academy would give him the discipline he needed, along with demanding academics.

David Maurice Robinson was born in Key West, Florida, on August 6, 1965. He has a sister, Kim, who is two years older than he, and a brother, Chuck, who is six years younger.

Young David was an intelligent student growing up in Virginia Beach, Virginia, where he had been placed in programs for gifted children as early as third grade. When he was a little older, he accompanied his mother to the grocery store and totaled the prices of her purchases before she got to the checkout counter. Later, in junior high school, he took advanced math and computer classes at a local college. "Learning was what was really important to me," Robinson said. "I tried to learn as much as I could about everything I did. . . . I just had an incredible curiosity."

He played piano, and he also played some sports, including golf, football, tennis, and baseball. Although he played all sports well, he excelled at none, except perhaps baseball. After Robinson had made his way to the NBA, his mother told sportswriter Brad Buchholz of *Inside Sports*, "It may sound strange to say this [now], but I always thought his sport would be baseball. He seemed to have everything you needed for baseball: He could run, he could throw, and he could hit. I still remember David's community league games;

he couldn't have been more than nine years old at the time. Every time David came to bat, the people in the stands would bet on him to hit a home run. And he could do it, too, either right-handed or left-handed."

The left-handed Robinson tried organized basketball briefly. He played sparingly as a 5-foot-9 student in junior high school, then quit the game. He didn't begin playing basketball again until his family moved to a Virginia suburb of Washington, D.C., where his father, retired from the Navy after 20 years, had taken a job as an engineer. David began attending Osbourn Park High School in Manassas, Virginia, as a senior.

Robinson's high school yearbook includes a picture of him munching on cookies.

Even then, having grown to 6-foot-7, he wasn't exactly enthusiastic about trying out for the varsity basketball squad. Robinson said, "I saw the coach [Art Payne] in the guidance counselor's office and he asked me if I ever played. I told him that I really didn't have much experience, but he told me to come out anyway." Robinson showed up at practice and was added to the team as a backup center.

Shortly before the school's first game, Robinson earned a starting spot when the regular center was injured. Robinson played well enough during the season to earn all-area and all-district honors.

Robinson attracted some attention from colleges

Robinson, in the center of the back row, was a starter for his high school team during his senior year. It was his first year of varsity basketball.

because of his height, but most recruiters considered him to be a project, someone who would need special coaching to become even an average college player. Naval Academy coaches traveled to see Robinson play only after they learned that the 6-foot-7 athlete had already applied to the Academy. Even then they weren't very impressed by the skills of the tall player on an average high school team.

Mike Dufrene, who played against Robinson in both high school and college, recalled, as Robinson began his final year at the Academy, that Robinson "was a skinny, 6-7 kid who did OK because he was tall. . . . To compare him then [in high school] to where he is now — that's something that should be on 'Amazing Stories' or 'That's Incredible.'" Osbourn Park lost as many games as it won, going 12-12, during the one year Robinson played for the team. Nonetheless, Coach Payne was impressed by Robinson's ability to learn. "He improved every single day. He probably improved more than any kid I ever coached. But at that point in his life, basketball didn't mean a lot to him," Payne said.

What mattered most to Robinson was getting a college education. He also wanted military experience. His top choices were the U.S. Naval Academy and the Virginia Military Institute. With a score of 1,320 out of a possible 1,600 on his Scholastic Aptitude Test (SAT), Robinson qualified for almost any college in the country.

He really didn't have a hard time making the choice, although his father encouraged him to consider carefully the five-year Navy commitment that Naval Academy graduates must serve. If Robinson decided to pursue a basketball career, the Navy obligation would interfere. "My father really is the only one who saw the player I could become.... He said to me, 'You sure you want that five-year commitment?' But my mother wanted me to go there, and I couldn't see myself as a pro basketball player. So I went," Robinson said.

At 6-foot-7, Robinson exceeded the Naval Academy's height restrictions by an inch. However, the Academy makes exceptions for up to 5 percent of the incoming students as long as they are not taller than 6-foot-8. Robinson was one such exception. Apparently no one thought he would continue to grow.

When he arrived at the Naval Academy in 1983, Robinson had to get used to the abrupt change in his lifestyle. As a plebe, as all freshmen at the Naval Academy are called, he took orders from just about everyone. He also followed a rigorous schedule, with several hours of classes in his degree choice of mathematics, classes in Naval history and weapons systems, a couple of hours of practice, and lots of homework. He once said homework came in two forms: too much and way too much.

"The first day is always the longest day ever,"

Like all midshipmen (the title given to male and female students at the Naval Academy), Robinson had to adjust to a rigorous schedule.

Robinson said. "At the end of it, we had swearing in and then we went back into [Bancroft] Hall. And then they started yelling at us and telling us where to go. Most of the day, they were pretty polite, but then they weren't polite at all. I remember thinking, 'What have I gotten myself into?' I didn't get much sleep that first night."

Robinson didn't show signs of turning into an excellent basketball player during his first year at the Academy. He sat out the first four games of the season after breaking his hand while boxing during physical education class. He didn't start a single game. Robinson

wound up scoring an average of 7.6 points and col-
lecting 4 rebounds in the 28 games he played. His
most promising statistic was his field-goal percentage:
he made 62.3 percent of his shots. Navy won 24
games that year, the first time the team had won as
many as 20 games in a season. With Robinson playing,
the Midshipmen, as Navy sports teams are called,
would see three more 20-plus-win seasons.

Even though he was destined to become Navy's best basketball player ever, Robinson didn't enjoy the game in his Plebe year. "Basketball was more work than fun," he said. "I just wanted to play so I could get my letter."

He got his letter. Robinson also proved himself to be quite coordinated for his height by getting an *A* in the gymnastics part of his physical education class. He participated in gymnastics through all of his growth spurts. The experience likely helped him to avoid the awkwardness that frequently comes with large increases in height.

The next year, Robinson started piling up impressive statistics. He played in 32 games during his sophomore year—his Youngster year in Naval Academy terms—scoring 23.6 points per game and grabbing 11.6 rebounds per game. He started to assert himself on the defensive end of the court, blocking 128 shots.

Robinson also took his team to the National Collegiate Athletic Association (NCAA) tournament. Having grown to 6-foot-11, he helped the Middies to a 26-6 record, which won the Colonial Conference title. Navy went to the second round of the NCAA tournament, beating Louisiana State University before falling to Maryland. It was the first time in 25 years that Navy had earned an NCAA tournament berth.

3
Uncertain Future

By the time his sophomore year was over, Robinson was starting to realize that he had an untapped potential in basketball. He traced that realization to a pair of games in a tournament at Carbondale, Illinois. He had scored 68 points in the tournament and had taken 31 rebounds. "It was the first time I got an idea of what I could do," Robinson said. He began to wonder whether he should stay at the Academy or transfer to another college and develop his skills for a professional basketball career.

If he transferred before his junior year, he would be free of his obligation to serve in the Navy after graduation. If he stayed, he would probably have to wait until 1992 to play in the NBA. Robinson seriously considered transferring.

Robinson's improved basketball skills thrust him into the spotlight.

"I'll have to think about transferring because I might be missing a great opportunity to play pro ball and make a lot of money," he said during the middle of the season. "Still, I don't see myself as a Patrick Ewing, and if I spent all my time playing basketball, I might not enjoy it. My father says basketball's a transient thing."

Robinson also said he felt he belonged at the Academy. He admitted that his experience there was contributing to his personal growth. "At first, everything seemed unfair: no radio, no TV in the hall, no McDonald's on Tuesday nights. But what you get at the end—the responsibility, the respect, the security—keeps you going. You learn to cope, not complain, and problems don't bother you after a while."

Ambrose Robinson agreed that the Academy was the best place for his son. "The biggest advantage is its academic structure and togetherness," he said. "It's his decision, but I hope he stays. He's so at home there he forgets to call home here."

In the end, Robinson and his family met with Navy officials, who hinted that Robinson might see a reduction in his military obligation after graduation if he decided to stay on. In the face of accusations that he had cut a deal with the Navy, Robinson said, "They said they'd be fair, that's all. You can assume that if they had showed inflexibility or heartlessness, I would have walked the other way." Robinson stayed.

As Robinson became a better basketball player and attracted attention from pro scouts, he had to think about transferring from the Academy.

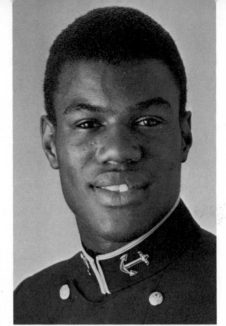

Left: Robinson shoots free throws in a game against Syracuse in the 1986 NCAA tournament. Right: Midshipman David M. Robinson as he looks in his dress uniform.

That summer, in 1985, Robinson played on a national team for the Jones Cup in Spain. During tryouts, he learned the merits of working hard from other players who were also trying to earn a spot on the team. "It was 105 degrees and these guys were busting it every day. They never wanted to stop playing," Robinson said. "It was kind of inspiring. I had to keep my mind in the games and play hard myself or I'd get absolutely killed. Even though we didn't win anything that summer, I really gained a lot of confidence."

He earned the national spotlight in his junior year, or as the Naval Academy calls it, his Second Class year, when he nearly led the Middies to the Final Four of the NCAA tournament. Navy was 30-5 that year and had won its second straight Colonial Conference title. Robinson was the center of attention.

27

He averaged 22.7 points and 13 rebounds per game. Most impressively, he set NCAA records for most shots blocked in a game (14), most shots blocked in a season (207), and most shots blocked in a college career (372). Only the entire national champion team, Louisville, had blocked more shots (213 total) than Robinson had blocked by himself that year. His rebounding and shot-blocking averages were the best in the nation among college players.

Robinson was named All-American by nearly every organization that compiles such a list, except by the two most prestigious of such organizations, the Associated Press (AP) and United Press International (UPI). They made their selections before Robinson came to national attention in the NCAA tournament. Both listed him on their third team All-America squads.

The Midshipmen, on the strength of a fine performance by Robinson, upset highly regarded Syracuse, 97–85, in the second round of the 1986 NCAA tournament. In that game, Robinson scored 35 points, grabbed 11 rebounds, and blocked 7 shots. In the next round, Robinson hit a basket with six seconds remaining to push Navy past Cleveland State. A loss to Duke in the Final Eight round ended the team's hopes of getting to the Final Four.

Robinson led Navy past Cleveland State in the 1986 NCAA tournament.

920499

As more and more people saw Robinson play and predicted success for him in the NBA, they wondered why he had chosen to attend the U.S. Naval Academy, and why he had decided to stay after his second year. Robinson might have wondered too, but he didn't look back.

His Naval Academy roommate and basketball teammate, Carl Leibert, told one magazine reporter that he never doubted Robinson would remain at the Academy. "A diploma from here means more to him than the millions he could have made," Leibert said. "He originally chose this place because he wanted something more than basketball and he stuck by his guns because he had made the commitment and that is the way he is. If he tells you he is going to follow through with something, it gets done."

Robinson showed a compassionate side of himself that year by befriending a young admirer. He struck up an enduring friendship with Clifton "C.J." Johnson when the 15-year-old ball boy for the Middies asked the team's star center to be his Big Brother.

July of 1986 brought more recognition to Robinson. He led the United States national team to a gold medal in the world basketball championship in Spain, winning the final game against the Soviet Union and its 7-foot-2 center, Arvidas Sabonis. Robinson outscored his taller opponent, 20-16, as the U.S. team won, 87-85.

Robinson's roommate, Carl Leibert, knew how much Robinson wanted to graduate from the Naval Academy.

His basketball accomplishments were merely a break from the rigors of Naval Academy demands. A month after the games, Robinson was training at the Quantico Marine Corps Base in Virginia, practicing war techniques. "We'd put our boots on by 6:15 in the morning. Next thing we knew, we were running through the woods, playing war," he said. "Six hours in the woods, creeping along at two miles an hour. Your back starts to hurt. You're sweating like a dog, then all of a sudden it starts raining."

Robinson had grown to 7-foot-1 by the time he began his senior, or First Class, year of basketball. Expectations for the team were lower than they had been the previous year because several players had graduated. Among the graduated players was Vernon Butler, a 6-foot-7 forward who had set Naval Academy records for career points and career rebounds. Butler's presence on the team had kept opposing teams from keying their defenses on Robinson.

Robinson had another adjustment to make. Navy had a new head coach in Pete Herrmann, who had been an assistant coach for Paul Evans. Evans had left Navy to coach at the University of Pittsburgh. In spite of the coaching change and the inexperience of Robinson's teammates, many publications had Navy listed among the top 10 teams in the nation.

Throughout the year, the media focused on Robinson's future. In the fall of 1986, Secretary of the Navy John F. Lehman, Jr., had allowed Navy football standout Napoleon "Cap" McCallum to play for the Los Angeles Raiders of the National Football League while the running back served with a Naval base at Long Beach, California. McCallum played in the team's home games, practicing each day after he finished his shift at the base. There was hope that Robinson might be given a similar arrangement that would allow him to play professional basketball part time.

When Navy officials allowed Napoleon McCallum, above, to play professional football and serve in the Navy at the same time, Robinson hoped they would let him play professional basketball while serving in the Navy.

Some people felt Robinson should have to serve the entire five years, because he had committed himself to the Navy twice—when he enrolled at the Academy and then again when he made a conscious decision to stay for his junior year. Others thought that, because he had grown so tall and could not serve on Naval vessels, Robinson should be released from any obligation.

Captain Albert Konetzni, Deputy Commandant at the Naval Academy, told *Sports Illustrated* that he would release Robinson if the decision were his to make. "If he wasn't a basketball player, I'd say to David, 'You have a pituitary problem. You've grown five inches since you've been here. You're not being commissioned. Here's your diploma. Bye-bye.'"

Partway through the season, Naval Secretary Lehman announced that because Robinson was too tall to serve on ships, planes, or submarines, he would serve the Navy for two years in a restricted capacity upon graduation from the Academy. After his two years were over, he would be free to pursue a professional basketball career, serving as a Naval reserve officer for a few weeks each summer for four years afterward. It appeared that if circumstances were right, Robinson would be able to play some professional basketball, perhaps during evening and weekend games. In order for that to happen, he would have to be stationed near the team that would draft him in June 1987.

Even with the distractions that came with those Navy decisions, Robinson had an outstanding season, scoring a total of 903 points in 32 games. His average of 28.2 points per game was third best among college players. His rebounding average of 11.8 was fourth. He was the national leader with 4.5 blocked shots per game. Robinson was named to the AP and UPI

All-America first teams and received all of the major College Player of the Year Awards. He was the only unanimous selection to the All-America first team named by the Associated Press.

By the end of the year, Robinson had added to his NCAA record for most shots blocked in a career, a total of 516. He also held 33 Naval Academy basketball records, including career points (2,669) and career rebounds (1,314).

In his final game of the year, against the University of Michigan in the first round of the NCAA tournament, Robinson scored a career-high 50 points.

Former UCLA Coach John Wooden, right, congratulates Robinson at a basketball awards ceremony. Robinson had just received the Wooden Award, one of several awards given to the top college basketball player.

Robinson moves to the basket in his final game for the Middies. He scored 50 points in a loss to Michigan to close his college career.

The gracious center left the game after giving way to a substitute with two seconds remaining and with no hope of Navy winning. As he walked off the court, fans gave him a standing ovation. Opposing players stepped over to congratulate him on an excellent game and his remarkable college career, and his own teammates gave him hugs. The standing ovation was the second of the night for Robinson. The first came after an announcement that Robinson had won the Naismith Award as College Player of the Year.

After Naval Secretary Lehman resigned, his replacement, James H. Webb, changed the policy that affected Robinson and McCallum. He said Navy officers would no longer receive special treatment to enable them to play professional sports. That meant McCallum would not be able to play football for the Raiders again until he had served his full five years with the Navy. Webb said, however, that because of his height, Robinson would still be required to serve just two years of active duty. He would not be allowed, under any circumstances, to play professional basketball during those two years.

Robinson received the news with mixed emotions. "I don't regret coming—this was the best place for me my first two years," he said. "If I'd known I was going to grow to be 7-1, of course I would have gone somewhere else. But things turned out for me real well the last two years and I can't complain at all."

4
Waiting

Robinson graduated from the Naval Academy on May 20, 1987. On June 22, a day that Robinson spent golfing, the San Antonio Spurs made him the first basketball player selected in the 1987 NBA draft. The Spurs knew he would be unavailable until the 1989–90 season.

Instead of joining the Spurs in Texas, the Navy's tallest ensign (the rank Robinson received upon graduation) was headed to southeastern Georgia.

In early July, Robinson reported to the King's Bay Naval Submarine Base, where he would be working as a civil engineer in charge of construction projects. He sat behind a desk most of the time, getting outdoors occasionally to check on different phases of construction.

Later in the summer of 1987, Robinson played on the national basketball team in the Pan Am Games.

The day before the Pan Am Games began, Robinson took time to answer questions from reporters.

The United States team won a silver medal after losing to Brazil. Despite the medal, the games were considered to be a disappointment, because the U.S. team had been expected to win. Critics pointed to the team's failure to live up to expectations as an indication that Robinson didn't have what it takes to play against professional basketball players. Robinson was in foul trouble during the whole game with Brazil and played only 15 minutes, less than half of the game. Even so, he scored 20 points, had 10 rebounds, and blocked two shots.

After the Pan Am Games, Robinson returned to the base to work, fitting in basketball training workouts at the gym whenever he could. "My conditioning was important. I'd get to work at 7:30 A.M. so I could take a two-hour lunch and lift weights. Then in the evenings I'd go to the court and shoot," he said.

If he needed more incentive to keep working out, it came in the form of a long-term contract with the Spurs in November. He signed an eight-year contract that made him an instant millionaire.

When the Pan Am Games were over, Robinson returned to his job at King's Bay Naval Submarine Base. Submarines and their support ships are frequently moored side-by-side offshore.

Most of the money he received right away from the Spurs was placed in a trust fund. Robinson could only take money from the trust fund to cover living expenses, such as food, clothing, and apartment rent, until he turned professional. This allowed him to remain an amateur to compete in the 1988 Olympics.

During the early months of 1988, Robinson attended special Navy training in civil engineering at Port Hueneme, California. He played in the Armed Forces basketball tournament, then went on a recruiting tour for the Navy in Washington, D.C., giving speeches at high schools in the area. It was the Armed Forces tournament that forced Robinson to step up his conditioning. In the tournament, he failed to start even one game because he was so out of shape.

He headed back to the Naval Academy to prepare himself for the U.S. Olympic trials, training under his old coach, Pete Herrmann. Herrmann had Robinson do wind sprints (in which he had to run up and down the court as fast as he could), distance running, weight lifting, and swimming to build up his endurance.

Even though he was out of shape, and critics thought he wouldn't make the team, Robinson had higher goals. "I want to go out there and be one of the best. I want to stand out," he said.

Although he hadn't played very much basketball for almost a year, Robinson showed flashes of greatness in the Olympic trials.

Robinson patiently answers questions from a swarm of reporters
during the Olympic trials.

The U.S. Olympic basketball coach, John Thompson, selected a small squad, made up of Robinson and other players trying out for the Olympic team, to tour Europe and play against national teams from other countries. The main purpose of the trip was to give Robinson some playing time so he could polish his game instincts and get into better shape.

As the 1988 Olympics in Seoul, South Korea, approached, sportswriters speculated that Robinson wouldn't make the team. His performances had been less than spectacular. Some sportswriters hinted that he wasn't motivated. Robinson tried hard to dispel any notion that he was taking it easy on the basketball court. "Every time you go out on the court, there's a pride factor. This is what I do. This is my job. This is what I'm best at. Every time I play, I play like I have something to prove."

However, Robinson admitted that he wasn't playing as well as he would have liked. "I didn't feel that much behind at the Olympic trials, but the more I play," he said, "the more I see about myself, the more I notice deficiencies that I'd rather not talk about. I'm only 70 percent of where I want to be."

Robinson had some trouble adjusting to Thompson's style of coaching, which did not emphasize any particular player. Despite all the reports about the drop-off in Robinson's level of play, one important person wasn't worried.

Paul Evans, who coached Robinson for three years at the Naval Academy, said Robinson simply needed to get used to a new system of basketball plays to be ready for the Olympics.

Bob Bass, at the time general manager of the Spurs, said, "I think the way John [Thompson] coaches, no one is going to get 25 points and 15 rebounds a game. He's playing a lot of people."

Even Robinson's old coach from the Academy, Paul Evans, came to his defense. "I think people are making too much of the layoff. This is a different system for him," he said. "When I had David, we tried to do what David did best. But John has 14 kids; he's got to do what's best for 14."

Robinson made the Olympic team, but the U.S. players placed third at Seoul, even though they were picked to win the gold. The criticism about Robinson's abilities and motivation started anew.

While other players from the squad returned to their colleges or went to play for their teams in the NBA, Robinson returned to King's Bay submarine base with the memory of defeat still fresh in his mind and a year to go before he could play in the NBA. "I try to put the Olympics out of my mind. It was real disappointing, and for a long time I blamed myself," he said. "It took a long time for me to get over it. I know, though, that I did the best I could."

5
New Spurs

When Robinson was discharged from the Navy on May 19, 1989, he immediately went to work with the Spurs. With special coaching from Brown and competition in summer leagues and the Midwest Revue for rookies, he polished his basketball skills.

In the meantime, with a little more time on his hands, he pursued other interests. He moved to San Antonio and bought a condominium for himself and a house for his parents. He moved a baby grand piano into his condominium and began to teach himself to play piano again. He also bought an electronic keyboard to take on the road when the Spurs traveled.

People were fascinated that this basketball player was able to play classical music, including Beethoven sonatas. Robinson credited his father with teaching him both to play and to enjoy music. "I grew up with classical music, which my dad had me listen to, and I learned to appreciate it a lot. That's what I started learning on the piano." The more he played piano, the more he began to experiment with other types of music.

Robinson's family — sister Kim, father Ambrose, brother Chuck, and mother Freda — attended many Navy games.

Robinson's relationship with his family has always been good. While he was in the Naval Academy, his parents frequently drove to basketball games in a car that had the license plate NA50VY (Robinson's jersey number is 50). Ambrose and Freda Robinson moved to San Antonio to help their son adjust to the demands of a professional basketball career. They handle many of his appearances, track his financial investments, and help him answer fan mail. By the end of his first year, they were sending out about 700 autographs a week. They attend all of the Spurs' home games.

In the fall of 1989, David's brother, Chuck, who had occasionally served as ball boy during David's career at the Academy, was admitted to the U.S. Naval Academy. Robinson said he didn't really encourage his brother to go to the demanding college. "It was very obvious to him that I learned a lot about myself there and that it was a good experience," Robinson said.

Robinson also said the Academy helped him to be self-motivated. "I really had to get pushed to achieve. My mother did the pushing. Where I'd be without her I don't want to think about," Robinson said. "But gradually, ever since I went to the Academy, I have felt my motivation growing."

Robinson noted that serving in the Navy had a positive effect on his basketball career. "When guys first come into the NBA after college, they not only have to get used to the pro game, but they have to get used to the lifestyle of being on their own. Well, I've had two years to get used to being on my own, and now my only real adjustment is to the NBA," he said.

Robinson has had more than a few demands on his time as an NBA player. He spends a lot of time talking to reporters and fans after each game, sometimes missing the team bus back to the hotel on out-of-town trips. Coach Brown used to ask Robinson if he would like the team to restrict the number of writers seeking interviews with him or the number of fans asking for autographs, but Robinson always manages to handle the situations by himself. "He's got time for everyone," Brown said. "What's terrific is that he makes people feel good."

In Robinson's rookie year, Nike unveiled advertisements that had him performing an imitation of the television show "Mr. Rogers' Neighborhood." In "Mr. Robinson's Neighborhood," the audience learns words like "transition game" from special guests, such as Coach Brown. Another Nike advertisement has Robinson defining "garbage" as people who are involved in drugs. He said people who are garbage should not wear the line of Nike shoes he promoted. "Mr. Robinson doesn't like garbage in his shoes," he said. "Mr. Robinson doesn't like garbage in his neighborhood."

In his television commercials, Robinson spoofs "Mr. Rogers'
Neighborhood."

The Spurs traded for Terry Cummings to provide a boost on offense, so they wouldn't have to rely only on Robinson to score points. Besides being an excellent teammate, Cummings shares Robinson's interest in music.

Robinson's main impact was on the basketball court. He helped the Spurs win 35 more games than the team had won during the 1988–89 season. In the two seasons Robinson had served in the Navy, the Spurs had posted 31-51 and 21-61 records. The 21-61 season was Coach Larry Brown's first with the San Antonio Spurs and his 17th season coaching either college or pro basketball. It was his first losing season as a coach.

Knowing that Robinson was coming on board the next fall, Brown pressed management for new players to complement Robinson's abilities and to take some of the pressure off the rookie player.

By the time the Spurs were done dealing, there were only three players back from the previous season. The Spurs had acquired veterans Terry Cummings and Maurice Cheeks. Cummings, from the Milwaukee Bucks, could score a lot of points. Cheeks, a point guard from the Philadelphia 76ers, could run the offense. The Spurs also had several young players in the starting lineup. Willie Anderson, one of the three players from the year before, returned for his second NBA season. Sean Elliott was the third pick in the 1989 NBA draft. Cummings, Cheeks, Anderson, Elliott, and Robinson formed the starting lineup.

In Cummings, Robinson found a kindred spirit. Cummings has sung background vocals on several gospel albums and plays the keyboard. The two spent time composing music during the season in San Antonio and while on team trips. Robinson also became known for other pursuits. Without regular practice, he consistently scores in the 190s in bowling. He likes working logic puzzles and playing Nintendo video games. He also became known for sneaking in golf games between daytime basketball practice and evening games. Robinson's golf scores are good—in the low-90s over 18 holes.

All of those stories helped to fuel the criticism about Robinson's concentration on the game. Robinson shrugged it off. "I knew coming in would be difficult, playing 82 games after not playing but 10 or 12 games total the last two years," he said. "I've been more consistent than maybe I would have expected."

The Spurs made an important acquisition in veteran center Caldwell Jones. Jones, in his 18th professional season, was brought in specifically to help Robinson adjust to playing center in the NBA. Robinson impressed Jones on the first day of training camp. "The man has unlimited talent. He runs, he blocks shots, he's smart, he does everything well," Jones said. Robinson, who was to have the benefit of Jones as a tutor for only one season, credited the veteran for helping him learn the finer points of defense.

Veteran center Caldwell Jones, who retired after the 1989-90 season, helped Robinson work on his inside game.

One by one, the other teams in the NBA learned how good Robinson had become. With the new players, San Antonio won 56 games during the season to set a new record for improvement from one season to the next. The 35-game turnaround was three better than the 32-game turnaround Boston had after Larry Bird joined the Celtics as a rookie in 1979.

Before long, the Spurs' newfound success was bringing huge crowds to San Antonio's HemisFair Arena. Near the end of the season, home games were drawing nearly 15,000 fans, about as many as the arena could hold.

Robinson swept all the Rookie of the Year Awards and was named to the All-Star team and the All-NBA third team. He was named the Schick Pivotal Player for his role in helping the Spurs improve. He finished the regular season tied for ninth among the scoring leaders, with a 24.3 average. He was second in the NBA (behind Hakeem Olajuwon) for rebounding, with 12 per game, and third in blocked shots, with almost four per game.

In the All-Star Game, Robinson played 25 minutes, picking up 15 points and 10 rebounds in a losing effort for the West team. East won the game 130-113.

Coach Don Nelson of the Golden State Warriors told anyone who would listen that Robinson deserved to be named the league's Most Valuable Player, even though the award hadn't gone to a rookie in more than 20 years. "I think David is the best player in the league this year. It's clear-cut for me. He should be MVP and Rookie of the Year. I can only compare David to a guy I used to play [with], Bill Russell. But [Robinson] is quicker," Nelson said. Bill Russell was selected as the "Greatest Player in the History of the NBA" by a panel of sportswriters in 1980 and was named MVP five times in his 13-year career with the Boston Celtics. Despite Nelson's endorsement, Robinson placed sixth in the voting.

More important to Robinson than any individual award, however, was the Spurs' performance during the season. In addition to improving its record to 56-26 (best in Spurs history), San Antonio beat the Utah Jazz in a tight race for the Midwest Division title. The Spurs breezed past Denver in the first round, then fell behind the Portland Trail Blazers, two games to none, at Portland. San Antonio won the next two games at the Spurs' home court to even the series. When the teams returned to Portland for the fifth game in the best-of-seven series, San Antonio played tough, battling back from 22 points behind to tie the game at the end. Portland pulled out a win in overtime, however.

The Spurs won the next game in San Antonio to force the seventh and final game. That last game also went into overtime, but the Spurs made a costly mistake with the game tied.

had done well. A good sign for the future was that the team had not relied completely on Robinson to win its play-off games. During the season, all of the starters averaged more than 10 points per game. Forwards Terry Cummings and Willie Anderson had stepped up to take control at crucial times during the play-offs.

Robinson's style of play had people comparing him to one of the best players in professional basketball, Bill Russell (6). Russell was both a player and a coach in his last three seasons with the Boston Celtics.

The Spurs came close to beating the Portland Trail Blazers in the NBA play-offs.

The Spurs appeared destined to be one of the NBA's best teams for years to come, and Robinson clearly was a candidate for superstar status by the end of his rookie year. Even his coach was saying as much. "David's gonna get better. This is just the tip of the iceberg. If he can learn to deal with 100 games a season and the attention he's gonna get, he can be the greatest," Brown said.

During the following season, his second, Robinson was getting better—showing improvement in almost all areas of his game. Then, in January, the United States declared war on Iraq. Robinson had trouble concentrating on basketball while some of his friends from the Naval Academy were in the Persian Gulf to fight. "It was obvious that I was very disturbed when the war first broke out," Robinson said. "It was hard to play knowing that this world event was going on. It made the game seem real insignificant."

The team battled other problems as well. Injuries kept key players out of the lineup throughout the season, and Terry Cummings and Coach Larry Brown openly argued. San Antonio captured its second straight division title, but had little momentum going into the play-offs. The Spurs lost to the underdog, Golden State, in the first round.

Even so, Robinson was an outstanding force on the court. He improved his shooting percentage, scored 25.6 points per game, and was the NBA's top rebounder. He also blocked more shots than any other player. In a year that saw Patrick Ewing's performance drop off, and in which Hakeem Olajuwon was injured for over a month, Robinson was the top center in the league. He was also one of the best players in the game. At season's end, he placed third in the voting for the MVP, behind Michael Jordan and Magic Johnson. Robinson clearly belonged in the NBA.

DAVID ROBINSON'S
BASKETBALL STATISTICS

United States Naval Academy

Year	G	FGs-at	%	FTs-at	%	rbds	blks	pts	ppg	rpg
83-84	28	86/138	62	42/73	58	111	37	214	7.6	4
84-85	32	302/469	64	152/243	63	370	128	756	23.6	11.6
85-86	35	294/484	61	208/331	61	455	207	796	22.7	13
86-87	32	350/592	59	202/317	64	378	144	903	28.2	11.8
Total	127	1032-1683	61	604-964	63	1314	516	2669	21.0	10.3

Naval Academy Records

1. Career points — 2,669
2. Points in a season — 903
3. Points in a game — 50
4. Career rebounds — 1,314
5. Rebounds in a season — 455
6. Rebounds in a game — 25
7. Career blocked shots* — 516
8. Blocked shots in a season* — 207
9. Blocked shots in a game* — 14
10. Career field goals made — 1,032
11. Field goals made in a season — 350
12. Field goals made in a game — 22
13. Career field goal attempts — 1,683
14. Field goal attempts in a game — 40
15. Career free throws made — 604
16. Free throws made in a season — 208

17. Free throws made in a game — 21
18. Career free throw attempts — 964
19. Free throw attempts in a season — 331
20. Free throw attempts in a game — 27
21. Career field goal percentage — .613
22. Field goal percentage in a season — .644
23. Field goal percentage in a game — 1.000
24. Free throw percentage in a game — 1.000
25. Career steals — 160
26. Steals in a season — 66
27. Career double-figure games — 98
28. Double-figure games in a season — 35
29. Consecutive double-figure games — 67
30. Career 30-point games — 30
31. 30-point games in a season — 15
32. Consecutive 30-point games — 3
33. Scoring average in a season — 28.2

*indicates an NCAA record

San Antonio Spurs—Regular Season

Year	G	FGs-at	%	FTs-at	%	off / def / tot	blks	pts	ppg	rpg	ast	pf	stl	to
89-90	82	690/1300	53	613/837	73	303/680/983	319	1993	24.3	12	164	259	138	257
90-91	82	754/1366	55	592/777	76	335/728/1063	320	2101	25.6	13	208	264	127	270
Total	164	1444/2666	54	1205/1614	75	638/1408/2046	639	4094	25.0	12.5	372	523	265	527

1990   NBA All-Star Team; Rookie of the Year; All-Rookie Team; Schick Pivotal Player Award; NBA All-Defensive Second Team; All-NBA Third Team

1991   NBA All-Star Team; All-NBA First Team; Schick Pivotal Player Award; NBA All-Defensive First Team

Key

G-games	rbds-rebounds
FG-field goals	blks-shots blocked
at-attempts	pts-total points
FT-free throws	ppg-points per game

rpg-rebounds per game	ast-assists
off-offensive rebounds	pf-personal fouls
def-defensive rebounds	stl-steals
tot-total rebounds	to-turnovers

ACKNOWLEDGMENTS

Photographs are reproduced with the permission of: Bob Peterson, 1, 53;
Phil Hoffmann, 2, 12, 20, 26, 31, 46, 50; Ric Vasquez/San Antonio Light, 6;
San Antonio Spurs, 9, 54, 56; Bill Gillingham, 11, 38, 60, 64; Osbourn Park High
School, 15, 16; U.S. Naval Academy/Phil Hoffmann, 19, 22, 25, 27; Bettmann
Archive, 29, 35, 36, 40, 43, 44; Phil Hoffmann/U.S. Navy, 33; CDR G.I.
Peterson/U.S. Navy, 41; Andrew Bernstein/NBA Photos, 48; Independent
Picture Service, 59; and San Antonio Spurs/Charles Cyr, 63.
Front cover photograph by Nathaniel Butler/NBA Photos. Back cover photo-
graph courtesy of PHC Jeff Hilton, U.S. Navy.